Stories of My Child Going Through . . .

The Terrible Twos

Copyright: February, 2019
by Michelle Lacroix

Welcome to the Terrible Twos!

That phase where your child can go from being an absolute angel to a hellion in the blink of an eye. . . usually when other people are around to witness the transformation!

Then there are the days when you don't think you'll have the energy to make it through the day until they fall asleep.

It's a tough stage; it truly is.

However, there are also all those bright moments when they do or say things that bring tears to your eyes.

The big squeeze/hug that comes
from nowhere with the accompanying
sloppy kiss on the cheek . . .

That "I love you, Mommy" moment
that tugs your heart strings . . .

And the stories . . .

Your little darling getting up in the
middle of the night and filling up the
fish tank with small toys . . .

Or trying to help Mommy by putting a
diaper on the dog . . .

How about brushing the cat . . . with
your toothbrush?

These are the little stories that need to be captured on paper for sharing later on in life.

Those little treasured moments that will bring back memories for years to come.

Family stories are best when shared by someone who was there! Whether you were the one who caught the moment or the one who had to clean it up later, writing down those moments, those stories, will provide pleasure for those who read them in later years.

Enjoy this journal and share those memories!

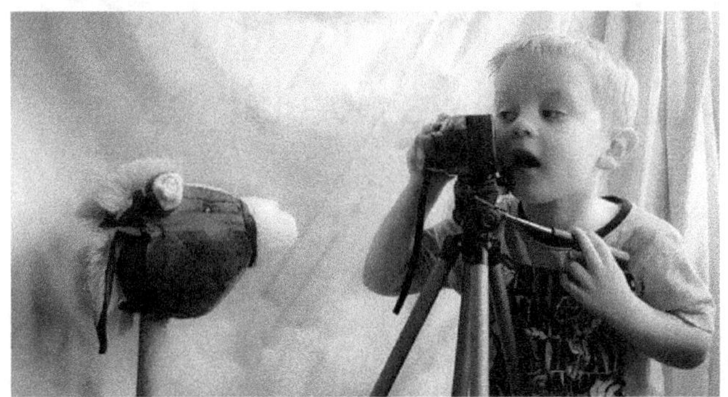

I'd like to take a moment to say "Thank you" for purchasing this book.

It is my hope that you will enjoy writing in this "The Terrible Twos" journal and truly find joy in jotting down your thoughts and memories while going through this phase in your child's life.

If you wouldn't mind going to Amazon and leaving a sincere, honest review about this book? As a self-published author, I would appreciate it as others may not find this book without good reviews available for viewing.

Again, thank you, and I hope you enjoy writing in your journal.

Best Wishes Always,
Michelle

Did you know I have other books available?

I have blank cookbooks and other journals for sale on Amazon under my own name, Michelle Lacroix. If you type my name in the search bar there, all of my books will be listed for you.

I also write children's books under a pen name, Jamie Nicolle. More about these books may be found at www.jamienicolle.com and on Facebook at https://www.facebook.com/MsJamieNicolle.

My children's books are available on Amazon in both Kindle and physical book formats.